THE EDGE

Creating a life of impact by unlocking the most important element – YOU

BRETTANY SOROKOWSKY
& CARLA HOWATT

By the Book Publishing

Brettany Sorokowsky
& Carla Howatt
The Edge
*Creating a life of impact by unlocking the most
important element* – YOU
All rights reserved.

By the Book Publishing
3 Donnely Terrace Sherwood Park, AB T8H 282 Canada
Brettany Sorokowsky
& Carla Howatt

Printed in the United States of America
First Printing 2019
First Edition 2019
ISBN 978-1-7751605-4-0

10 9 8 7 6 5 4 3 2 1

Library and Archives Canada Cataloging in Publication
The Edge; Creating a life of impact by unlocking the most important
element - YOU Howatt, Carla
Sorokowsky, Brettany
Sherwood Park, AB Canada

THE EDGE

TABLE OF CONTENTS

Introduction

"All with Grace"

~**Carla**

The idea for this book was birthed over a cheap bottle of Malbec, amidst the barking of a dog and the squeal of a two-year-old. At first, we thought we were writing a blog post, but then it quickly morphed into something much bigger. Like our lives, it grew and spread and ended up resembling nothing we thought it would when we first started.

We wanted to share our stories of succeeding as women in business, but we soon realized we had more than one or two stories to tell and that those stories might resonate with many women. As two women who have faced a lot of adversity in our lives, we knew we had a lot in common, but it was only as we began digging deeper that we realized just how different we were as well.

You see, Carla was born into a world of hippies and flower power, while Brettany never experienced a world where the Berlin Wall was still up. One was raised in a traditional family with a stay at home mother and the other had two working parents. They approached life from two very different starting points.

Even with those differences, it soon became apparent that we shared life experiences that taught us similar lessons and gave us a shared vision of the world. This vision included one where we are responsible for taking what life throws us and doing with it what we will. We have both learned lessons about the world and about ourselves that have helped us thrive in business.

At 32 years of age, Brettany's work history has included helping to establish a $25 million resort and managing it. Between the ages of 16-21, she sold and flipped real estate and at 19 years was the youngest platinum seller in a multi-level marketing company, earning $100,000 a year. She created a business called the Blood Sugar Stabilization Clinic that helped more than 1000 people and earned her a nomination for Alberta's Female Entrepreneur of the year in 2012.

As if that wasn't impressive enough, Brettany also established Canadian Development Strategies Inc., the only privately-owned investment company in Canada.

Carla walked a different path and she went from being a single teenage mother on welfare to becoming the founder of two communications companies, the creator of a publishing company, the author of three books and became an elected official and well-respected leader within her community.

Working through our vision of the book, we started taking notes on what made our success possible. We started talking about what message we wanted to impart and how we wanted people to feel while they were reading it. It became apparent that an overlying theme would be grace. By that, we acknowledged that we are all at different stages in our lives. In whatever stage we are in, we have varying degrees of ability and readiness to understand, perceive and process life's lessons. There is nothing to be gained by beating ourselves up about lessons we should have learned years ago or even a month ago. We will learn when we are ready and when we are at a point in our life where we can accept those truths.

This book is not intended to be a memoir of our lives but rather stories of our lives that lay the foundation for the reader to understand that we know what it is like to have times when life just smacks you in the face and you are left stunned and unsure how to deal with it.

Throughout the good times and the bad, we have learned lessons in life and business that we are passionate about sharing with other women and leaders.

Chapter 1

"Love Never Fails, Character Never Quits."

~Brettany

BRETTANY - I grew up in a pretty idyllic setting; we lived on a farm just outside of a small town and only one mile away from my Dad's parent's farm. I still cherish the times I spent with my grandparents and recall riding on the school bus my grandpa drove every day. I would keep him company and giggle from my seat when we would plow through the snow, clearing the way for others.

Family values were at the core of everything we did. Life was lived to be enjoyed and shared with those you love and care. Community was also a large focus in our home; without the community coming together we could not achieve everything that was needed to when you're a farmer. I remember all of us chipping in to help the neighbor during harvest or calving. "A rising tide raises all ships" was something I heard a lot of in our house.

As a child, I was a gatherer of all things that didn't have a family. My mission was to give all these creatures a safe place. This meant that I had lots of cats to keep me company and even adopted a stray family of skunks after finding them motherless by the train tracks. I was an observer as a child and I didn't talk until I was almost three. This was cause for great concern and my parents and doctors had me tested for everything from celiac disease to cerebral palsy. My parents were thrilled to find out that I simply needed my adenoids removed and tubes in my ears.

My parents were big dreamers and had decided they wanted to raise my brother and me according to the old-time farmer's values. I loved living on the farm with my 30 cats, two dogs, 250+ head of cattle, goats, milk cows, a beautiful brook and miles of fields to let my girlish daydreams run wild.

My Mom, who was born in 1962 and was three years younger than my Dad, was an occupational therapist who traveled almost an hour and a half one way every day to go to work. When my Dad wasn't working hard on the farm, he was a contractor and built homes and commercial spaces in Edmonton. Together my parents built their family of creation. Their focus was first on ensuring that they had a strong relationship with God, a healthy marriage and that their kids would become good adults; a legacy of love. Parenting became very intentional when my Mom realized that my brother and I were very different. What worked for one didn't always work for the other. I was a quiet a submissive child and my brother was a sensitive, strong-willed child. A career for my mom would be birthed out of her passion for being a peacemaker for families who had sensitive strong-willed children.

As part of my intentional childhood, our family would always be guided by a mission statement - a grid of truth for which all our decisions were filtered through. The first one that I remember is: *With God as our co-pilot there is nothing so great that we cannot get thru it together.* This was not a constantly changing statement and I only recall two during my childhood and we took it seriously and still do to this very day. I believed this is a foundational piece of emotional discipline that my parents taught my brother and me.

My parents raised me to work hard and with the belief that whatever you get out of life is what you put into it. One of the cornerstone moments in my life was when I was in kindergarten my parents took one of our bulls to a show in the USA. When they were at the show, our bull was injected with a venereal disease. They didn't realize it at first and brought the bull back to our farm where it spread to the rest of the herd. In the end, my parents had to slaughter the entire herd and sell the farm to avoid bankruptcy. I remember sitting on our railway tie fences and watching these men load all of my beloved friends (cows/bulls) onto semi-tractor trailer units and driving away. After this disaster, my family was unable to support ourselves living on the farm and we moved into town when I started grade one. One of the things I learned from this experience was that everything can come and go so quickly.

Moving to town was not positive for me and I made sure my parents knew it. Gone were all my cats and a carefree childhood and in its place were rules and constraints. No longer able to roam around freely, I now had to be supervised and boundaries around our yard were established. The move also took me away from my grandparents and that was something that was devastating for my six-year-old heart. My brother and I made the best of it by catching frogs and selling them to our fellow classmates, many games of kick the can and my beloved cat Snowwhite (My favorite cat from the farm that my parents let me bring to town with me).

The next several years of my childhood my family spent paying the debt of the farm off. My parents built a large MLM business in their off-hours from their careers. Their work afforded us to pay off 1 M in 6 years and enjoy many fun trips all around North America. In the time left over after working and building a business my parents ensured that my brother and I had hobbies - for both of us, it was sports – I played basketball and my brother played baseball. Free time was not something we had an abundance of, although we did make moments along the way. My parents worked hard at meeting the needs of the home. There were no formal gender roles; whoever had the time to do what needed to be done, did it. This helped my brother and I see that life is by your design. You do not need to live based on other's expectations of you. Life is a canvas and you are the artist.

After we finished paying off the debt of the farm our money efforts then went to creating a family counseling center. My mom was busy putting together everything she had learned through her formal education, additional training and life experience of raising my brother and I. This birthed "A New Day Begins… - Helping one family at a time" The focus of the center was sensitive, strong-willed children and parenting. With the success of A New Day Begins, mom launched her radio show "One Family at a Time." Looking back, I know that A New Day Begins was my mom's passion project and she poured everything she had into helping each and every family that walked through her doors. This sometimes led to a feeling of jealousy and envy; I wanted her focused attention. I didn't want to wait for her to finish reading the faxes or returning messages. I started to help her in the office just so I could have quiet moments with her all to myself. The struggle for me was always to be mature enough to extend grace to my mom as she helped thousands of families come together through love.

It was also around this time that our family mission statement changed to "*Love never fails, character never quits*". While our previous statement was appropriate for the difficult times we were going through, it was time to move on and our mission statement reflected the new direction we were taking as a family. It spoke to our desire to show character in all things, to honor our commitments, work hard and be kind.

My childhood was filled with open doors, possibilities, dreams, hard work and sacrifice. This is part of the foundation that has led me to pursue what I believe to be true. I have never felt the need to live within the confines of the pressures of society. Without this foundation, I wouldn't have been open to some of the greatest opportunities for joy in my life. I would have spent life making sure I followed the "right" path of life, but instead I had the privilege of living a purpose-driven life full of love, joy, and intention. I wouldn't be writing this book with my dear friend Carla, I wouldn't be sharing with you in the following pages some of the greatest "keys" to the success that I have been able to learn. Let me also share this with you - Success is not dollars in your bank account; success is being able to finish well. Finish well with your partner, with your children, with your soul.

"If money is the solution; you don't have a problem"

Family Mission Statement

For a long time, I took for granted the fact that my parents raised our family with a mission statement. I just assumed that every family had a mission statement that used as a guiding document when making decisions. When I realized the truth — that most people don't have their own personal or family mission statements — I was a bit flabbergasted. I wasn't confused as to how they were able to make decisions in their lives if they didn't know what was important to them and had nothing to guide them in life.

It wasn't long that I began to understand that people were floundering for those very reasons; they hadn't taken the time to really think about and articulate what was important to them and what they wanted out of life. They didn't have a grid of truth. "How can you build a firm foundation on a bed of sand?"

QUESTIONS TO GET YOU THINKING

☐ What things are important to you in your life?

☐ If you were to die tomorrow, would you wish you had done something that you haven't already?

☐ If you weren't afraid of failing, what would you try?

☐ What ten words would people use to describe you?

☐ Do you have a mission statement or a statement of truth that you use in your daily life?

CHAPTER 2

"Do you want a run-of-the-mill obituary?"

~Brettany

CARLA - I often say I was born in the oil fields and raised in the wheat fields of Alberta. I was born in Fort McMurray in 1966 when its population was 2,000 hardy souls. I don't have many memories of life in 'Fort Mac' during the eight years I lived there except for playing with kids on the muddy road of our trailer court and visiting my cousins.

We moved to a smaller town in north-central Alberta when I was eight, joining my mother's parents. It was here that I spent the next ten years of my childhood.

My parents had what would definitely be considered a traditional marriage based along gender roles. My mother stayed at home to raise me and my two siblings and my father headed off to the plant to work. Vacations including heading to Manitoba to visit my aunts, uncles and a plethora of cousins from my Dad's side of the family. My family was a 'wait until your Dad gets home' type of family that was very typical of the '60s and '70s.

I remember one time, I had done something wrong, I don't even remember what it was, but it was bad enough that I knew I was in deep do-do. As in big trouble. Somehow my mother had found out about it and sat me down to talk to me about it. I was crying, my mother was letting me know in no uncertain terms that I was in trouble. I recall quite vividly sitting on the steps going downstairs and talking with her. In between sobs and wiping the snot off my face with the back of the shirt of my arm, I hiccoughed a request.

"Please don't tell Dad!"

Because I knew that as much trouble as I was in with Mom, it was nothing in comparison to what was going to happen when Dad got home from work and found out. I don't think I will ever forget what she said as it really highlights some of the differences in the way she approached parenting and her marriage compared to many people today.

She looked me in the eye and told me that she would not keep any secrets from my Dad. She explained that she would be married to my father long after I was raised and left home and that she would never jeopardize her relationship with him by keeping secrets.

When I tell people this story, some are surprised that I was not insulted, but I heard it as a statement from a woman who was very clear on her role as a mother and as a wife. That conversation has stuck with me over the years and I often reflect on how unusual that perspective must have been during an era when women revolved their lives around their children and their role as a mother.

There were a lot of ways that we were raised as a product of the times; my brother was told to be a big boy and stop crying, my sister and I had our hair put in ringlets and wore bright pink hotpants. If we did a somersault on the front lawn, we were admonished for showing our underwear with a "for shame!".

Don't get me wrong, I had a wonderful childhood full of hot summers spent biking around town, playing pranks on Halloween and walking down the railroad tracks to make a fort. Our parents never seemed to worry about us or even wonder where we were – not because they were negligent, but because in those days, they didn't have to worry about the things we worry about now. I would wake up every morning to the smell of coffee percolating in the glass coffee pot on the stove and a blue haze of cigarette smoke drifting near the ceiling. It was just a different, more innocent time.

When I was eight or nine, an incident with a relative left a permanent scar on my psyche. Although I am choosing not to go into details in this book out of respect for people in my life who are still alive, it is important to understand that it shaped many of my behaviors and actions for years to come. In fact, I believe that one of the ways it impacted me the most was that when I hit my teens, I started looking for love in all the wrong places - so to speak. Okay, to be more accurate, it was looking for love in high school. As a result, I was pregnant by age 16.

Finding out I was pregnant during the summer of 1982 was definitely a shock. I had known girls who had been sleeping with their boyfriends for a while and here I was, pregnant after one encounter. My devastated parents talked with me about my options and whether I would keep the baby or give it up for adoption. I recall being shocked that there would be any question, but I went through the motions of considering giving up my baby for adoption.

My memories of that time, oddly enough, don't include much worry or anxiety. Sure, there was the usual teenage angst of relationships and worry about my rapidly expanding waistline, but I don't recall being concerned about the future. I had a baby shower and set up a crib in my bedroom, scoured books for just the right baby names and waited patiently for the big day. I knew my parents thought I had ruined my life before I had even got started, but I mentally and emotionally brushed that thought aside. Of course, I would go on to do what I wanted with my life and I would do it with baby in tow.

After a pregnancy of much drama, tears and upset, I gave birth to a bouncing baby boy who weighed nine pounds and eleven ounces. My Mom drove us home from our four days stay at the hospital with my new baby safely cradled on my lap. It was still a very different time.

I was now a newly turned seventeen-year-old girl with a brand-new baby boy and another year and a half left of high school. I will be forever grateful that my parents loved and supported us both. My mother watched my son while I attended school and graduated with my high school diploma. It was only the fall after I graduated from high school that I really started to think about what life had in store for me. My friends were heading off to college or university and I stayed behind, waitressing at the local diner. I was suddenly very alone. My son's father was working in the big city and only came home on the weekends. I was living in a small, mice-infested guest house behind an old house on the highway. I would get up in the morning to get ready for my shift at the diner and trudge, rain or shine, down the highway to take my son to the sitters so I could walk back and be ready to start work on time.

Before long, I found myself out of work and on welfare. I quickly realized I needed to make some real plans for my life. I had applied to a journalism program at a local college and was accepted, but reality soon set in. There was no way I could take the courses and put in all the extra time that would be necessary while toting a toddler around. Although I had always wanted to be a journalist, I did not pursue my dream. I applied to take a clerk-typist course in the city and soon moved there with a friend who was also a single mom.

I soon married the father of my son and we moved to the suburbs. Another son was soon on the way and then five years later we had a daughter. Both pregnancies were healthy and went off without a hitch. It was only a few hours after my daughter was born that the hospital realized something wasn't quite right. My daughter was born with Down syndrome and two holes in her heart.

I recall that time as being full of tears and uncertainty. I loved my daughter ferociously, but I was grieving the loss of the daughter I thought I was carrying. We were lucky in that over the course of the next few months, one of the holes in her heart started closing and the second one began to grow shut. In the end, she would not need surgery.

When my tiny, undersized daughter was five years old, she became diabetic. Type one diabetes is only controllable by insulin injections and I had to learn how to inject her and do finger pokes while she cried. I struggled to know how to fit her diabetes into how I viewed her future independence. Teaching her to be as independent as possible would be a struggle as it was, but throw in blood sugar levels, drawing syringes of insulin and regulating food made it a hundred times more complicated, as well as raising the stakes immensely.

For the next eight years, I raised my children as a stay at home mother. I took in a few kids here and there in order to bring in extra money, but for the most part, I was the picture suburban housewife. I traipsed around the countryside taking the boys to hockey practices, hockey games and to visit friends. I participated in speech therapy, occupational therapy and physical therapy with my daughter. I sewed pink frilly dresses for my daughter and created bright, colorful blankets designed to stimulate her mind.

In 1999, I decided it was time to go back to school and I enrolled in a public relations program at the local college. By the time the course was over, so was my marriage. There are always many reasons why a marriage fails and it is never just one person's fault but he summed it up when I left by saying that when

I went back to school and he was left to deal with making meals and cleaning the house, he knew he didn't need me.

This divorce, for a person who was raised with a mother who was so clear that she would be with her husband for the rest of her life, was a devastating failure. I was the first person in my family to separate and go through a divorce. In fact, I am the only one to this day. My parents have been married for sixty years, my brother for about thirty and my sister over twenty-five. We had only made it seventeen.

It took me quite a while to come to terms with my divorce and I dated very little for the first few years. My oldest son left home and my other kids were spending half the time at their Dad's house. For the first time in my life, I was living as an adult, by myself and in a home, I had bought. The divorce was devastating but the freedom was exhilarating. I spent the next several years taking care of myself. I re-discovered what I liked to do on the weekends, I stayed up late reading if I got too engrossed in a book, and I left the guilt at the door. I decided to try new things and my proudest accomplishment during that time was to take up running and to participate in four half marathons in three different countries in 18 months. I lost a bunch of weight, discovered a love of mountain biking and hiking and participated in several women's support groups that enabled me to really go deep into issues in my life. In short, I really learned who I was.

WHO ARE YOU?

During the ten years that I was single and on my own, I had an opportunity to really learn who I was and who I wanted to be in my life. Before that, I had coasted through life, and let life happen to me. When I reflect now, I realize that I had little choice in the matter; I didn't know who I was and I didn't have anything to guide my decision making. I also learned that because I didn't know myself, I didn't always effectively interact well with people in my world.

How could I articulate what I wanted out of life and out of my relationships if I didn't even understand and know what made me tick and what I wanted? I had never given any thought to what type of relationship I wanted within marriage so how would I know if I would be satisfied with taking on the traditional role of wife and mother? The answer is, I didn't know. So, I married my high school sweetheart because he was the father of my son and because I thought that was the next step. I hadn't considered that I had other options or that it might not make me happy.

Without the ability to know and understand myself, I was a raft afloat and at the mercy of whatever wind blew.

Questions to Get You Thinking

☐ If money and time were not a consideration, describe your ideal life?

☐ If fear and common sense were not a consideration, describe your ideal life?

☐ What do you wish was not part of your life right now?

☐ What is your biggest fear in life?

☐ What are your top five strengths?

☐ What would your friends say are your top five strengths?

☐ What did you want to be when you were a teenager?

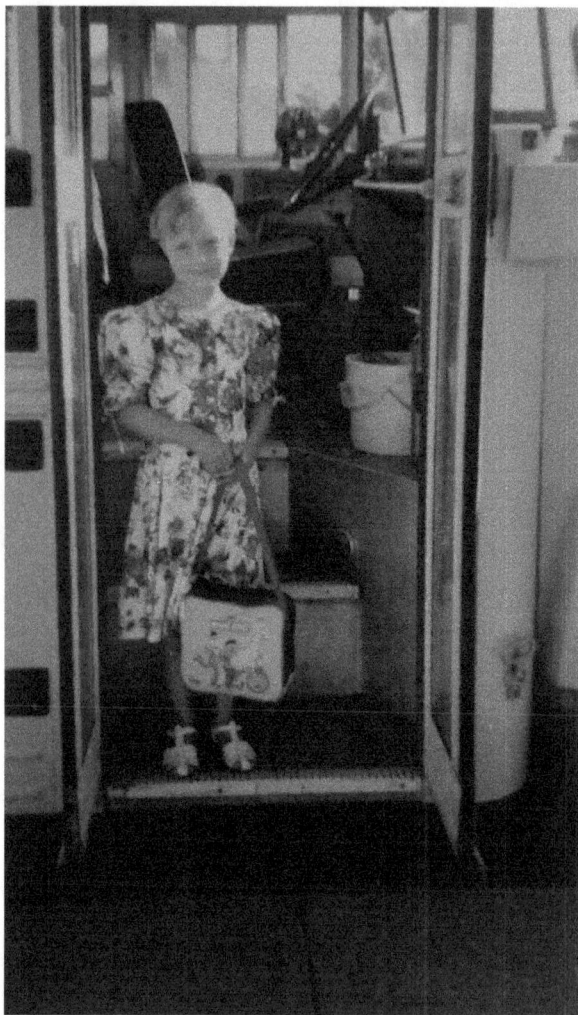

A school-aged Brettany on her way to school.

Co-author Carla at seven years old

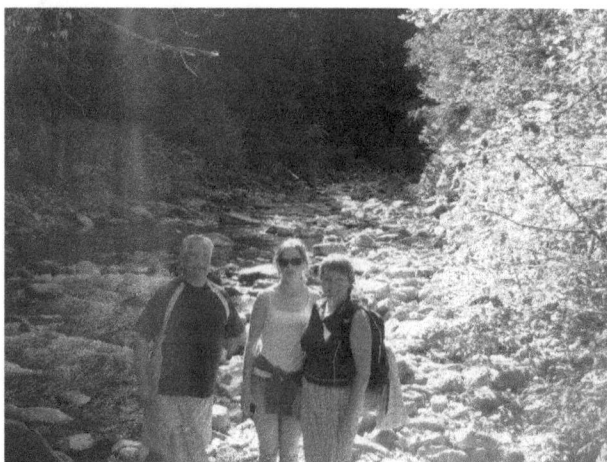

A teenaged Brettany with her parents

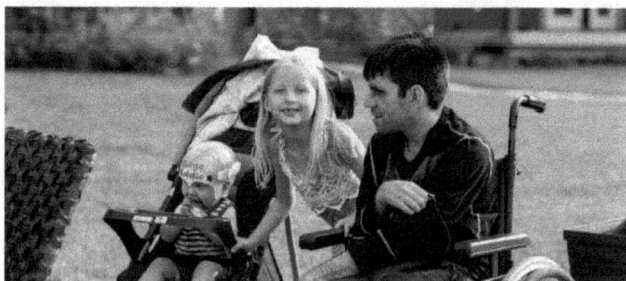

Brettany's children enjoying life on their farm after
her son's Craniosynostosis surgery.

Carla's high school graduation picture, taken when her son was a year old.

Brettany when she was dating Greg

Brettany and her chosen child, Justin

Justin

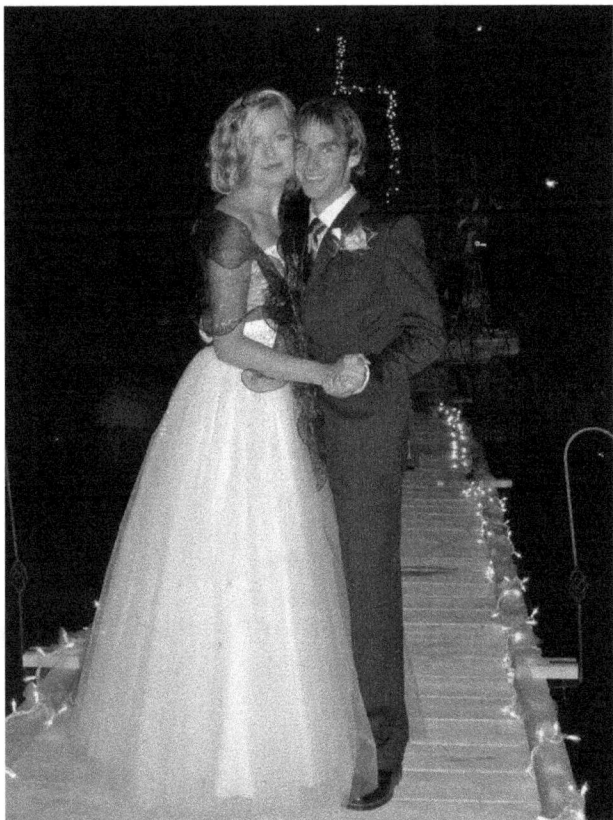

Brettany marrying Russell amongst their family and friends.

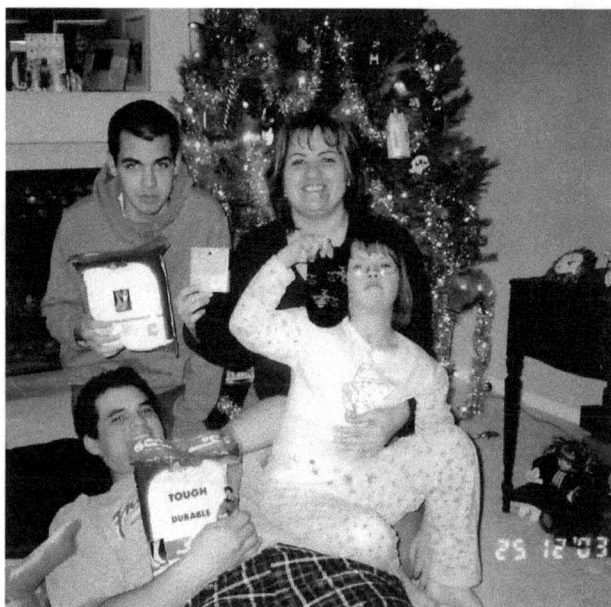

Carla celebrating Christmas with her kids during her single years

The peace and power is in God – Brettany writing on the Florida beach shortly after Greg died.

Carla marrying her second (and last!) husband Don

Carla's son Adam who took his life in 2015, at the age of 27

Carla's parents celebrating their 50th wedding anniversary

Carla signing her oath of office as a brand new
council member

CHAPTER 3

"Beauty comes from ashes and flowers in graveyards"

~Brettany

BRETTANY - I was in grade ten when I met someone who would change my life forever. He would change how I viewed the world and how I moved in it. His name was Greg. He was smart but shy. He was a skater dude with a dark side who loved punk rock. I fell head over heels in love.

Greg was three years older than I and he was even taller. For a young sixteen-year-old girl who was six feet tall, this was magical. He was also mysterious, and I was attracted to this dark side of him. I realize now he had a sad soul. As soon as we started seeing each other, our relationship found its focus: sex. Neither of us were big drinkers, and we didn't do drugs, but we found our addiction in each other's bodies. The pull I felt towards him was something I didn't know was possible and I realize now that it wasn't overly healthy.

Every chance we got, we were renting a hotel room and we planned our time around where and how we could have sex. I was young, I was naïve, and I thought he was the love of my life. When I first met him, he was a nerdy, gangly boy who stood 6'5" tall and was definitely not the cool kid in school. Within months he started acting like he was a rock star. He partied hard, throwing outrageously large parties that were loud and disruptive. At one point a police helicopter was called to break up one of the parties. Because of this drastic change, his friends blamed me for being a bad influence on him.

What his friends didn't realize was that his father's death, a few months after we started dating, had hit him hard. He had inherited a large sum of money and he was intent on spending it. It was not unusual for him to buy $100 steaks and $1000 bottles of tequila. We went pub crawling in fancy limos and at one point he took all his friends on a large vacation to Disneyland. Again, I thought this was normal behavior and if I needed money for something, all I had to do was ask him and he would peel off bills and hand them to me. His friends knew he was spending a lot of money, but I don't think they saw the whole picture. He was living at home and spending ten to twelve thousand dollars every month. I was an immature, sheltered teenager living a fast-paced adult life and I had no idea just how in over my head I was.

During this time, my mother was working hard at her counseling career and my father was occupied by building custom homes. They knew Greg wasn't a good influence on me and they wanted to get me away from the situation, but they weren't sure how.

My family and friends warned me that the relationship wasn't good for me and it did not fit into what I had always said I wanted and how I had lived my life. But I was young, dumb and in love. Throughout the years we were together, our relationship was on again and then off again and full of drama. Eventually, Greg began attending post-secondary to become a civil engineer, but he was failing the majority of his classes.

Looking back, there were red flags that things were going downhill for him emotionally. I recall him telling me once that he loved me but I would never be enough for him and that he would always need other women. His preoccupation with sex and porn intensified. Early in November, when I turned 20, he threw me a birthday party that was even more large and lavish than usual.

In 2005, I noticed a charge on my credit card that wasn't mine. I looked into it and discovered he had charged my card for purchasing pornography. At first, he denied it and I wanted to believe him but I knew deep down he was lying. At that point, the issue for me was not the porn but that he had used my card without my permission.

Then, in the middle of November 2006, I took my computer into the store to get fixed. The people who worked at the store found child pornography on the computer and called the authorities. I was never told exactly what they found, but in retrospect, I believe he had filmed us together. Because of our age difference, I was considered a child. The questions they asked, the way they treated me, was more of a victim than of a criminal's girlfriend.

Victim services mentioned that I was in an abusive relationship and used words like turbulent. Where did they come up with the idea, that our relationship was abusive unless they had found videos and realized he was taking advantage of our relationship? I still believe there may be videos of me that he sold and that linger on the internet today.

On Nov. 30, 2006, earlier in the day, Greg told me that he 'loved me until the end of day,' which I thought was odd because we never said I love you, we always just said 'until the end of days,' but I brushed it aside and let him know that I would be hanging out with a girlfriend that night.

Later that night, one of Greg's friends called to find out if Greg was with us. He was concerned when he heard we were alone; he had a bad feeling about Greg. My friend and I jumped in a car and drove towards the city to try and find out what was happening. We were half-way there when we received a phone call. Greg was dead.

It is as though my world went blank. Things slowed down to a crawl, while simultaneously speeding up. It seemed to take us forever to get where he was, but suddenly we were there. He looked like he had so many times in the past, as though he had gone to sleep while listening to his music, this time sitting in the driver's seat.

The next thing I knew, I was in the backseat of an ambulance and I could hear my friend telling someone that I had no one. While I realize now she was saying that I had no one to come and get me, at the time I heard it that I had no one anymore. Greg was gone and I was alone. I had no one.

After some phoning around, they were able to connect with my brother and he came and picked me up. It was in the dead of winter and Greg's body had frozen so when they removed him from the vehicle, he was in a sitting position. My brother shielded me from seeing Greg's body being removed and for that, I am very grateful. I learned that Greg had left a suicide note behind that said if the world wanted him to live, then Brettany would find him in time. And if I didn't find him in time, it was until the end of days. In essence, the note spelled out that his life, or death, was on my shoulders.

The next couple of days were a blur and then my parents took me to Florida. I don't recall much about that trip, not even why we were there. I don't know if it had been planned before Greg died, or as a result of his death. I don't know if it was a business trip or a family vacation. I just know I was heartbroken. I was angry at my parents for taking me away and I stayed in our hotel room and ordered lobster through room service. I thought by doing so I was teaching my parents an expensive lesson.

Because we were in Florida, I was not able to go to Greg's funeral. I was furious at my parents for keeping me away. I was mad at the world and I was mad at Greg. But oddly, I didn't feel I was entitled to my grief. I was, after all, just the girlfriend. I felt like I couldn't talk to my parents about what had happened because they had warned me that he was bad news and I didn't listen.

I was still in touch with victim services and they were watching me closely, concerned that I may become suicidal. I never considered killing myself but I spent a long time in a super dark place, not functioning properly for quite a while. When I returned home, victim's services would call me every week and meet with them for coffee to reassure them I wasn't suicidal.

I found no help within my social circle either. I was the girlfriend of the guy who offed himself. Was she the one who made him do it? Was all this her fault?

The police were involved you know, were they investigating her? Was it really a suicide? The rumor mill ran rampant and the theories got crazier and crazier. I was left with anger, rage, numbness and an attitude that no one was going to hurt me ever again.

I began seeing a counselor twice a week and continued doing so for the next two years. I learned so much about myself and about the world around me.

I learned you have to respect the choices other people make, whether you agree with it or not. In the end, the choice to take his life was his choice to make. It wasn't an easy process; the emotional bondage that suicide comes with is one of the most horrific things I may ever have to handle. But I also learned that I didn't have an option. My whole life would have been messed up if I didn't deal with Greg's demons.

I remember vividly when I learned how to release that demon; I kept having a dream of being in a room, standing on cold, sweaty cement, completely naked. The dream happened night after night until I realized that the room was my grief. The room was the box of grief that I was stuck inside. I needed to let it go.

Once I realized this, I experienced my first feeling that I could live again.

This point in my life has left a very big mark on me. The time I spent with Greg, my brain was still developing. It was during a formative time in my life and we were keeping a lot of secrets. I often wonder if that is why I don't share a lot with other people. Keeping things quiet became an ingrained way of life.

CHAPTER 4

"We all just want to be heard and be known"

Carla

BRETTANY - A year and a half after Greg's death, I started dating my future husband, Russell. I was still struggling with Greg's death and I blamed myself for his death. It would be years before I would understand that I was not responsible for what had happened. I met him through my Mom's business and at first, I thought he was an arrogant know-it-all. As time went by I began to realize to see the kindness in him. We had fun together doing things like cooking, traveling and dreaming.

Less than a year after we began dating, we were engaged. A few months after our first anniversary together, we married. I was only 22 years old, but I had never been surer of something or someone in my life. Russell and I shared a belief in creating the family we dreamed of. Our vision was to create a family that dreams, laughs, works, plays and loves together.

Russell and I were both fully aware that we came from very different backgrounds and very different experiences. We wanted our differences to bring us together rather than pull us apart.

That is not to say it was smooth sailing, not by a long shot. I had trust issues after Greg, as well as some irrational fears. I was afraid when the phone rang or whenever Russell was late for something. I felt I needed to do whatever it took to keep Russell happy and content. If he wasn't happy, I panicked. I still felt that Greg's death was my fault so it only followed that if I did anything wrong in my relationship with Russell, that he might do the same thing.

It took years of weekly counseling for me to dispel these feelings and Russell was supportive and encouraging; he came to counseling with me when we married and pointed out when I was behaving irrationally. Bit by bit I began to heal and trust in our relationship.

These types of experiences, so early in our relationship brought us together even closer. The dynamics of our family relationships drew us even closer; Russell was told by his family that he did not have their blessing to marry me. They also talked down about him to me whenever they had the chance. While Russell has worked hard to try and establish a healthy relationship with his mother, he has, to date, not been successful. These relationships helped to mold and define our relationship as husband and wife by showing us that family is not just what you are born into but it is what you create. We have had the opportunity to define our family of creation, while at the same time honoring our family of origin.

While Russell and I were intentional about establishing our family, we for sure had to learn some of the lessons the hard way. We laughed and we cried - we stood together through it all. This is one of the greatest gifts Russell has given me. He loves me without expectation. Life does not need to be perfect, life needs to be real. Real Life for each and every one of us looks different, the goal is not all to be the same because that is just BORING!

CHILDREN

In 2007, before Russell and I started dating, I had purchased a condominium because I was preparing to take on the responsibility of a man who was very important to me. I was Justin's caregiver for years and knew that he was meant to be in my life forever. He had medical issues that included seizures, sleep disorders, and autism. Part of the government's requirement for me taking Justin into my home was that I had to own my own home. According to Nova and Gage, Justin is my chosen child. He has been a blessing beyond measure in my life. I simply do not have the words to express the love and gratitude that I have towards Justin and Justin's family of origin. My life is forever better because of all of them.

In 2010, Russell and I held our beautiful baby girl and welcomed her into our family. She was our shooting star and we named her Nova Rose. There is something to be said when you hold your first baby, just moments after they take their first breath. Nova has been my greatest teacher. Full of empathy and compassion, she has an innate understanding of how the world operates on a deeper level than I have yet been able to experience. Our Nova is an old soul whom it is a privilege to have the opportunity to parent.

Six years later, I gave birth to our son Gage. He was, of course, beautiful. When I look back at pictures of him, I can see he had a bit of a pointed forehead and an oval that was prevalent when you looked at him from above, but hey all babies have a face only a mother could love, right? Right?

Two months after Gage was born, we took him in for a checkup and the doctor said he couldn't feel a soft spot on the top of his head. He sent us for a second option and a week later, a pediatrician confirmed that Gage's soft spots were fused. This was the first time Russell and I heard the word craniosynostosis. My body went numb with shock, fear, and grief.

We learned that our sweet little boy would need surgery. They would begin by laying him on his tummy, then they would make an incision from one ear to the next and pull back his scalp. They would make a hole in his scalp and begin to take his scalp apart. The skull would then be remolded and put back into place. This was just for the back. They would then flip him over onto his back to do the same thing on the front, as well as remolding the forehead. It would take three neurosurgeons and 40 ccs of blood to do the surgery.

I can't put into words what it was like the night before his surgery. We had a large supper, that to me almost felt like the last supper. Somehow, we made it through and the next day we headed to the hospital and turned our tiny, sweet little man over to the doctors. To date, this was the hardest moment of my life as a mom.

Gage made it through 6-hour surgery and was soon outfitted with a helmet to help his head retain shape. We were so grateful to the doctors, nurses and the hospital where he underwent his surgery. Our lives hit full speed ahead during this time. We were occupied with multiple doctor's appointments each week, constant monitoring of temperature, insuring that Gage was never lower than a 45-degree angle and caring for a 16-inch incision that seemed to take forever to heal. In August we received the news that we could say good buy to the helmet and weekly appointments in exchange for every 6 weeks of monitoring by the neurosurgeon. I was ecstatic, we could maybe get our feet back underneath us - God had a different plan

In September we came home to a voicemail from Justin's pharmacist letting us know that his anti-seizure medication had been discontinued and that I should get an appointment with his doctor for a new prescription. I had no idea that this phone call would be the beginning of a three-month drug withdrawal. Russell and I would take turns every 3 hours to make sure that Justin was safe. My heart broke watching Justin go through hell as the drugs left his system. I was so scared for his safety, his quality of life and his health. We began to see elements of the real Justin begin to appear 8 weeks into the transition and I am happy to say that we have a happy healthy Justin sitting with me right now as I type these words.

With the reality of Justin maybe needing to be in a wheelchair full time, we began to look at how we could modify our home to be able to best care for all five members of our family. Little did we know that there would be a much bigger plan the universe had for us and we were introduced to a farm that would be one of the biggest leaps of faith we had made to date. Our reality was simple: Justin may be in a wheelchair for the rest of his life, Nova was struggling with huge obsessive behaviors and anxiety after the health challenges that both Justin and Gage had just gone through, and we simply do not know what will be the result of Gage's brain being squeezed. These were all harsh realities that Russell and I had to face head-on.

To face these challenges, we wanted to bring our children back to nature - the greatest teacher of them all. To get them back into nature we bought a farm. Life changed big time - we all had to go on a learning curve. Life became about working together to achieve something greater than any one of us could do alone. We went from living in the suburbs to owning farmland, a coal hopper, multiple rentals, and an Airbnb!

Through it all Russell and I have chosen to communicate. Even when it is hard and when it is uncomfortable. We learned how to celebrate what really matters and to leave the drama at the door. Without doing life together neither one of us would be where we are today - personally or professionally.

Life is better because we invested the first two years of our marriage learning our truth and how to communicate our individual needs while respecting the needs of the other.

COMMUNICATION

It had taken me going through the tragic and traumatic relationship with Greg for me to understand that I didn't want to go through another relationship like it again. I knew when I met Russell that I would have to learn how to communicate better within a relationship and I would have to learn how to open myself up again. Neither of these things was easy for me.

I learned how sometimes the way I was communicating with Russell actually had the opposite effect to what I wanted. My style was sometimes responsible for shutting down any chance for us to communicate effectively. I often thought I was being open and helpful when in fact I was closing the door to connecting in a deeper way.

QUESTIONS TO GET YOU THINKING

☐ When are you most receptive to hearing someone's opinion?

☐ When do you feel the least receptive to hearing someone's opinion?

☐ When was the last time you asked a question and then waiting quietly for the other person to answer?

CHAPTER 5

"Some people were just never taught basic manners"

~Carla

BRETTANY - The Airbnb was a success and we enjoyed being hosts. However, leasing out the shop was not going as well as we had hoped. The man had rented the shop to open a diesel mechanic's shop but we soon noticed that he was sleeping there as well. After being late with the rent a few times, compounded with him appearing to use it as his residence, we decided it was time he left. Before he could move though, he was thrown in jail. The police would not tell us what it was for and we were at a loss as to what to do. Because we were guardians of Justin, we could not have someone around who had a criminal record and we certainly didn't want him around the rest of our family either.

Unfortunately, he had other ideas and when he was released from jail, he used our address as his house arrest address. I had to move into a hotel with the family in order to make sure we did not put our children at risk. We also asked him to leave and when he refused, we went through the courts to obtain a restraining order. Once we had the order, we thought our problems would be over.

It didn't work out like that.

The renter – we'll call him John – began to send my husband and my father texts that were threatening and full of name-calling and vulgarity. He said he knew the Hells Angels and they would come for us. Our home was vandalized, and he would come by with his friends and part on our driveway. When we called the police, they said there was nothing they could do about it. One policeman went so far as to bring John up to our house and tell me that I should speak to him and try to get it settled. The policeman told me that I was being too dramatic about everything.

This went on for months. Our daughter was waking up in the morning to puke because of her nerves. She was afraid in her own house. Our friends were worried about our safety and we often left to stay at our family's cabin. We even went to the media in an attempt to bring some sort of attention to the issue. After the story hit the news, the threats intensified and we showed up at the police station, only to be told that because we had 'muddied' the water, they couldn't do anything. We involved our local elected officials and eventually, they arrested John and threw him in jail. For a few hours.

It took months for the police to finally take us, and our restraining order, seriously. Some additional training was mandated for the officers and the officer who was responsible for bringing John up to speak to me was disciplined.

Our family will never be the same again. When your basic safety is put at risk it puts a fear like no other into you. I had never known this fear, I had always had food, shelter, and safety. We lost our safety and our home at the same moment. My heart starts racing just thinking about this time in our lives. My heart goes out to anyone who has ever felt like their basic needs are in jeopardy. If this was ever you, I am sorry that you have felt this way in your life, you are worthy to feel safe and secure.

My reality is that what I believed to be true is in fact not true. I believed living in a first world country with a police force and a democracy that people had someone looking out for them. That when I called the police they were actually going to help. That the justice system puts the bad guys in jail. This is simply not what I discovered, I never have had to verify and justify as I did dealing with the police and the justice system. There are so many holes, failures, and shortcomings that I discovered I feel like I would need to write another book. It simply is your job to educate and represent your needs in this world. You do not need to be aggressive in your approach but you better be assertive.

ROADBLOCKS TO COMMUNICATION

My experience with the renter from hell reinforced that there are so many ways that we put up roadblocks to effectively communicating and dealing with each other. We do this within intimate relationships, but we also can do it within a business relationship – whether it be a colleague, client or customer.

I could go on for days about the dysfunctional way our renter communicated with those around him, but that would be too easy. He is an extreme example of someone who used bullying, threatening and accusing as a way of shutting down any meaningful interaction. However, it reminded me that we all block communication at times by using some version of these roadblocks.

I know I have been guilty at times of trying to solve a problem for a friend when all she really wanted was someone to listen to her. I have given her advice when she just wanted to be heard. I have accused my husband of something before I truly heard what he was trying to tell me.

QUESTIONS TO GET YOU THINKING

☐ When people have problems, do you want to solve it for them?

☐ Do you name call when disagreeing with someone?

☐ Do you shower people with praise, even if they don't deserve it?

☐ When is the last time you interrupted a person?

CHAPTER 6

"I can only slay one dragon at a time"

~Brettany

CARLA - I had one serious relationship before I met my husband and it was a disaster. I had been on my own for so long, I fell hard for the first man to show me attention and give me compliments. I put up with more than I should have and stayed months longer than was sane. By the time the relationship was over, my hard-earned happiness and self-confidence had practically vanished.

When I met my second husband, I was so happy to find a man who could make me laugh. He was funny, nice and adored me; what more could a woman ask? He shared with me his health history which included a benign brain tumor that required surgery several years prior. He saw a doctor every year for an MRI and each year the results came back saying there was no additional growth.

I remember when we took our vows, I teared up at the for "in sickness and in health" part because I knew that if things had turned out differently, he would not have been standing in front of me saying "I do".

Throughout the years after my divorce, my middle son had struggled with his mental health and developed addictions as a result. In the first five years of my second marriage, he came to live with my new husband and me. He had a suite in our basement, and it reassured me when I could hear him moving around down there. When he had been on his own, it would sometimes be days and weeks before he would reach out to me to let me know he was alive.

During the time he lived with us, we went through one piece of drama after another. He was caught driving impaired, he hit a parked car and then ran from the scene and hid it. He lost jobs and went through rehab. I tried everything I could think of from helping him to tough love. We lent him a car to get to work, only to have him take it out of our garage to joyride when we were on holiday. At some point, I began to emotionally pull away from the situation. He was an adult and I couldn't be responsible for his behavior.

I worried about my son constantly and one day the thing I had most concerned about happened. I had been out of town on business and when I returned on July 19, 2015, my husband and I found him in our basement, dead of a self-inflicted gunshot wound. He was 27 years old.

I remember screaming and running, sobbing into the phone with the emergency dispatchers before throwing my phone at my husband for him to talk. I ran outside and my next-door neighbor came running, he knelt down at where I lay in a crumpled heap on our front deck. He asked if it was my son and I managed to nod yes. He went into the house and helped my husband while his wife took me to their house.

It is hard to explain how it affects you when you go through something as traumatic as finding your child dead. My life is now separated into two parts before he died and after. Suddenly, anything was possible; my husband could die on the way home from work, my diabetic daughter could have a low blood sugar reaction and be gone in a flash. The world seemed so scary and menacing. I used to love traveling but now I was anxious. I operated with a low level of anxiety running through my body at all times, constantly on the lookout for the next horrible thing to spring on me.

My life as I knew it stopped. I was holding on to sanity with both hands and my feet were no longer under me. The world kept spinning but I just wanted to get off of it. At the time my son passed away, I was two years into a four-year term as an elected official. I struggled in my position as I had no emotional reserves left to deal with the negativity that people throw politicians way.

It was a few months after my son's death that I noticed my husband was really struggling. He had not been employed for several months prior to his death and he seemed to be sinking into a depression. He spent most of his days sitting on the couch and watching TV or flipping through Facebook on his laptop. He was there when I left for work in the morning and was there when I came back at the end of the day. His moods were dark and his attitude was negative. It was only when he had his checkup in April 2016 that we discovered his brain tumor had begun to grow again, twelve years after the first one.

We did the round of doctors and made preparations for surgery.

When he underwent brain surgery in November, I was concerned but also numb. I knew there was a chance that I could lose him and so I shut down some of my emotions. I told myself that if he died, I would be ok and it would be nice to be single again. I would go on a trip with some of the insurance money and things would be just fine. I look back now, and I am shocked and appalled at my cavalier thoughts, although I logically realize it was a coping mechanism as I couldn't imagine losing him, especially so soon after my son.

My husband's surgery went well, and he was released into my care the next day. Unfortunately, they forgot to give him steroids to control the swelling and within a couple of days, we were in the emergency department. It all began when I was waiting for him to get into the car so we could go and have lunch. He was just standing there, not moving. He couldn't get his body to listen to his brain. I hurried him over to the passenger side of the car and then went around to the driver's side and told him to shut the passenger door. He just looked at me with fear in his eyes and did nothing. I quickly realized he couldn't do it. I shut the door and drove very quickly to the nearest hospital. He could barely answer the questions the nurse asked him. We were soon whisked in to see a doctor. After some tests and a phone call to the neurosurgeon who performed his operation, he was pumped full of steroids. Over the next few hours, he gained some color in his cheeks and he was able to start answering questions. I knew he was going to be ok when he started cracking jokes.

He healed well after that and I was looking forward to having my husband back again. He would feel better, get up off the couch, be able to drive and soon find a job. But it didn't happen like that I'm afraid. He was better and he could drive again but he seemed in no hurry to find a job. He was not quite as down as before the surgery but he was still unmotivated. It was now going on four years of this and I was tired. Tired, stressed, grieving and fed up.

I finally confronted him and told him he would have to leave. I didn't want a divorce, but he would have to find another way to support himself and another place to live. He was shocked and upset. I went to our room and cried. I didn't want to lose him, but I was falling apart, bit by bit. I didn't have an ounce of strength left in me. Not emotional, not mental, not physical and certainly not spiritually. I felt defeated by life.

It was a turning point for us. He came to me and confessed that he could no longer read. That his memory was very bad and he thought he might have dementia. He told me that dealing with life was like driving in the night in the middle of a snowstorm with your car lights on. The world came at him like the snowflakes, fast and dizzying. That is how he experienced life now.

I couldn't understand how or why he had kept it from me. And I couldn't believe I hadn't guessed. I began looking for help immediately. I didn't want my husband to move out and now I had a better idea of what was going on.

We were able to get him a consultation with the local brain injury association and he was diagnosed as having a mild form of aphasia (difficulty reading and processing what you are reading, usually occurring after a stroke). The association was able to give him tools to cope with life such as the ability to enlarge the print on his phone so there were fewer letters on the screen and more whitespace. He went to the doctors and was prescribed anti-anxiety medication and anti-depressants. After years, I finally felt like I was getting my husband back and it felt great!

On Dec. 23, 2018, I spent the day preparing for Christmas. I was cooking and baking all day and setting the table so I would be able to relax and enjoy Christmas with my family and friends. After all my work was done, I sat down at my computer to check my emails. All of a sudden, an odd sensation rolled over my body and I instinctively knew something was wrong. I called to my husband and he came into the office, took one look at me and grabbed his cellphone to call emergency and let them know his wife was having a stroke.

In the end, I had two strokes that hit three places on my brain. I was in the hospital until they released me to my husband's care the night of December 24 with strict instructions to go home to bed and to rest. I was shaken to my core. It had never crossed my mind that my body might let me down or rebel against me. People around me became sick, not me. The medical profession was at a loss to explain why I had a stroke.

I wasn't old enough for that to be the cause, I didn't have a family history, I didn't have high blood pressure or a heart condition. I was overweight and stressed out though. I was struggling to support us on my salary, and it had been a really rough few years. I went through an incredibly low point where I just wasn't sure what to do. People told me it was probably a 'wake-up call' and I wanted to scream at them. A wake-up call to do what? Stop worrying about money? Not care about the health of my family? What was I supposed to be waking up to?

I had been taking care of myself to the best of my ability. I tried to meditate – with varying degrees of success – I loved floating in the sensory deprivation tanks and did it whenever I could afford it. I tried to get out and visit friends, what else was I supposed to be doing that I wasn't?

I decided to look for a salaried position and give up on the consulting business I had been running. I reasoned that a steady paycheque would be better than hustling for the next client. I found a contract part-time position that I was told would become permanent fulltime in six-eighth months. I started the work and for the first time in a long time felt that life was turning around for us. Until April. That is when I received a phone call from my daughter.

It was 7:30 am and she had been awake since about 2 am. She had received a text in the night from someone trying to scam her. It said that they were in the neighborhood and wanted to see her and they provided a link. She clicked on the link and saw what she will only tell me was "sex stuff". Her innocent mind was thrown for a loop and she sat in her darkened home, looking out the window, petrified that they were coming for her because they said they were in the neighborhood.

By the time she phoned me, she was traumatized. It would take months for her to get back to anywhere near her normal self. She had to move home, she needed a reminder to shower, to wake up, and to do her diabetes care. She had been so independent and now she was helpless and needed full-time care. She stared off into space as though in a stupor and tried to leave the house in the middle of the night because she said she needed to go save her friend.

Shortly after this happened, the organization I was working for changed the board of directors and decided that they needed to post for the position I had been promised. I soon found myself out of even a part-time job.

Something odd happened right around the time all of this was happening. I was okay. Yes, I had moments of feeling devastated. When was this going to stop? When would we be able to enjoy a nice, ordinary and boring life? But I was able to quickly pull myself out of it. The job? Well, the way the organization had handled it showed me that I was not interested in working with them as we would have soon been butting heads over the differing visions we had for how things should be run.

My daughter? We were able to get her help, she was living with us so I could keep an eye on her and get her health back on track. She is now feeling so much better and we are that much closer as a result.

CHAPTER 7

"Massive, imperfect action; expect turbulence"

~Brettany

BRETTANY & CARLA - While we are from two different generations and were raised in two very different families, there is much in common in our stories. Both of us have come to recognize the importance of knowing, understanding and respecting who we are and our own truths.

As we talked about our lives and worked through our stories, we realized that there were a lot of common threads. The commonalities we discovered were things that we know are what helped make us successful.

EMOTIONAL INTELLIGENCE

Both of us are very aware and tuned in to how we are feeling and oftentimes, why we are feeling that way. The fact is, if you have what is referred to as high emotional intelligence, you are more apt to identify issues and strengths and work them to your advantage.

This step might seem obvious and many people think it happens automatically. It might surprise you to learn that many people are not emotionally aware. For example, they may mistake fear for anger and lash out at those around them. Or, they may become defensive instead. By misunderstanding and misinterpreting their own emotions, they stay stuck.

It is much easier to deal with fear when you can identify that you are frightened. Once you have been able to identify the problem, you can take whatever steps are necessary to combat it. Or, as they say in alcoholics anonymous… "The first step to recovery is admitting you have a problem."

Emotional Intelligence is also choosing when not to react. This is one of the hardest and most important elements of leadership. The goal should never be to correct another individual's behavior, it should be asking yourself how you could reposition your behavior, tone or body language to produce the desired result. Leadership is not management. Leadership is a practice. As individuals we have not been placed on this earth to judge or convict we have been placed on this earth to love and empower. To love is a choice and to empower is a skill that few have developed.

SELF-TALK

While being emotionally self-aware is very important, what you do with that knowledge is even more critical. Let's stick with the emotion of fear. If you identify that you are afraid to expand your business, that is the first step. The next is to figure out what stories you are telling yourself yourself – are you telling yourself to not even consider expanding your business because if you do, you will just fail and lose everything? Are you going through a list in your head of all the times you have tried new things and failed? That is one way you might react. Or, you could acknowledge your fear, dig a bit deeper and ask yourself what the worst-case scenario would be if you expanded your business. You might respond that you risk losing everything. The next step is to determine if what you are afraid of is likely to come true. And if it did come true – so what?

When Brettany was sixteen and flipping houses, what was the worst that could happen? She lost everything she had. Ok, so what?

She was sixteen and she had plenty of time to make mistakes and experience failure. It truly would not have been the end of the world.

"The only person who will be with you in birth and in death is you"

The ability to acknowledge and address our internal self-talk is imperative to any individual. It is even more important to an individual who has influence. I have always used the saying that your business is only as big as you are. I am not referencing the size of your shirt but the size of your heart. It is a simple reality that you cannot help another if you cannot help yourself. The first place we can help ourselves is by being our own best friend.

I (Carla) have learned over the years that I am much more successful if I get out of my own way. I am the one who puts limitations on myself by the way I speak to myself, by the beliefs I have about my personality, my skills, and my abilities. For example, I realized in one of those shocking epiphany moments that I viewed myself as a person who doesn't and won't make a lot of money. I would get by and I would be okay, but I would never be one of those people who have 'the big bucks.'

This has stopped me from pursuing larger opportunities and settling for smaller ones.

This epiphany came to me when I invested in a business coach for the first time. He asked me some probing questions and I realized I was mentally pushing back at what he was telling me because I didn't believe it was true for me. Yes, maybe hard work and planning could help others have majorly successful businesses, but that was not me. My coach looked me in the eye and asked me the very pertinent and apt question – what made me think I was so special? I still chuckle when I think of that moment.

Learning from someone who had been there – business-wise – helped me to see things clearly and realize just how much I was letting the story I told myself shape how I was running my business. It was time I started learning from others – who knows, maybe I could learn from other's mistakes instead of creating my own?

We have had some lemons thrown our way in life - and not because we were bad people or because we did something to deserve the crap that landed on our laps. We had to learn how to know our own truths and then remind ourselves on a regular basis that we have enough, we do enough, and we are enough... This is the habit of self-talk. We need to control the narrative or else the narrative will control you.

Through everything that has transpired in our lives we have discovered that the victor is love. We both have had the privilege to be raised in homes full of love, we both have husbands that love and adore us, we love the differences in one another and we choose love over all else.

CHAPTER 8

"Resilience Breeds resilience "

~Carla

BRETTANY & CARLA - One of the things that we have in common is an ability to bounce back, no matter what it is that life throws our way. This resiliency is part personality and part determination and an understanding of what it takes to build a life where resilience is fostered and encouraged.

What we call the *resiliency edge* is something that has enabled us to go on in the face of tragedy, challenges, and adversity. This is sometimes confused with strength because it can look like we are strong in order to get through things. The truth is that strength is the easy part. It is easy to get through things by grinning and bearing it, but the hard part is to make it through a difficult experience and emerge in a positive place – which, incidentally, is how we define resiliency.

Some things in our childhood and upbringing fostered resiliency, and some things didn't. Brettany was raised to believe that if she had a clear plan and focused on it, that she could do anything. Love conquers all. Carla was told that she could do anything she set her mind to and her parents instilled in her a sense of personal responsibility.

The truth is that the more you experience and learn resilience, the more resilient you will become. Getting through a bad situation and coming out the other end is an experience that will teach you how to bounce back and thrive; this makes it that much easier to do it instinctively the next time. Resiliency is a muscle you work. You can practice your resiliency muscle everytime you come up against a challenge. Work that muscle by identifying how you feel when faced with it, determine what stories you are telling yourself, re-write those stories, and find a solution. If you practice this process on small issues that arise, you will be ready for when the big ones show up.

So why is resiliency so important in business? You can have the brains, skills, the ability to manage money and people but if you aren't resilient, it won't matter. Why? because it can make or break you as an owner.

Think about it – in order to keep going when you are floundering in your business, when the bank is looking for a loan payment or you just lost your biggest client to your competition – what does it take? It takes resiliency. If you don't have resiliency, you will curl up into a ball, you will assume the victim role and go nowhere. However, if you are resilient, you will take decisive action and deal with things.

Of course, you don't have to be resilient every moment of every day; sometimes you just need to acknowledge your feelings and deal with them. Because resiliency is not about sticking your head in the sand and pretending everything is ok when you know it isn't, it is important that you acknowledge and deal with the very real emotions that can come up during a crisis.

Part of being emotionally aware is realizing when you just need to cry, rant, rage or even whimper. It's ok to experience those emotions, but it is equally important that you move on from them and don't let them immobilize you or make decisions. So, go into your bedroom and punch a pillow or bawl into it, go for a rage walk and call whoever needs it every name in the book (in your head, not in directly to the person!).

When you have calmed down and can deal with things productively, you can start flexing your resiliency muscles. Even if you have a strong emotional reaction and a need to fall apart at the beginning, that does not mean you have failed or that you are not resilient. It is what you do with those emotions and how you proceed which will determine your success.

Remember, resiliency is not a badge of honor to hang on your wall, it is the quiet strength where you know you are going to be okay no matter what happens. This is a muscle that you can rely on.

CONCLUSION

Your true strength is in the moments where you are vulnerable with yourself and with others. So many people want to live in the Instagram moments or the high times of their lives but life is lived in the moments in the middle. Just like the poem The Dash - It is in the middle that counts. It is not the wedding day or the funeral but it is all the moments in the middle.

We want you the live your best life in the middle, we believe that business is a beautiful way to contribute to society. You create jobs, you spend money, you give money. Business is a point of high impact and we want to see worthy women making a real impact on the world. In order to get a high impact, the world needs worthy women.

We believe you are one of those women; we want you to be one of those women.

We have not shared with you our life stories with the intention of it being a comprehensive memoir because it only skims over some of the challenges and successes we have faced in our lives. Some of our personal, professional and business challenges and successes were touched on but are not the full story as that would take many more pages and chapters. The purpose of laying out this outline of our lives is to show the different roads we took to end up in the same place.

So, where did we end up? We ended up with the tools we need to thrive no matter what the situation. We have a well-thought-out statement for what we want out of our life and it guides us as we make decisions in our personal, business and professional relationships. We have a self-awareness that helps us deal with not only our own emotions but helps us interact with others in a productive and healthy manner. These are all building blocks to being successful in our lives and in business. We are able to establish boundaries, interact in productive and self-honoring ways while highlighting our skills and talents.

ABOUT THE AUTHORS

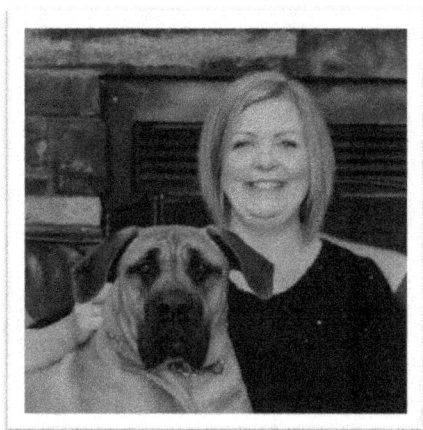

Brettany Sorokowsky

Brettany enjoys keeping life real with her husband, three lovelies, two dogs, many cats one horse on their farm in Northern Alberta. While still enjoying her passion for business by consulting and real estate investing, Brettany is loving the opportunity to invest and empower fellow female entrepreneurs.

Carla Howatt

arla lives in Alberta, Canada where she helped raise four children, two husbands and a pug. She a passionate about helping people live life in a positive way that enriches the lives of their community. A communicator at heart, Carla is also a proud introvert, port inhaler and dark chocolate hunter.